What Is AI?

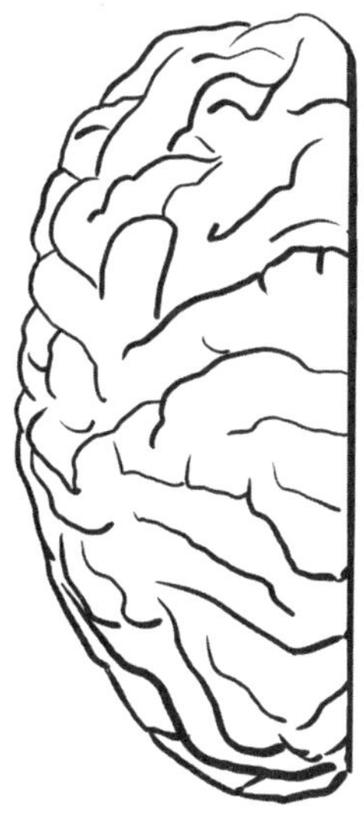

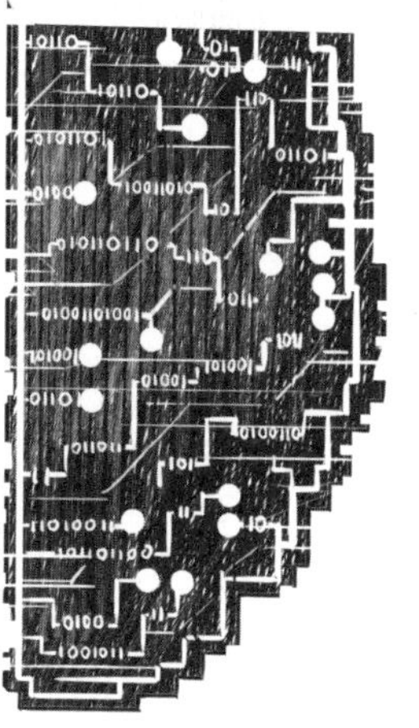

by Wes Locher

illustrated by Dede Putra

Penguin Workshop

To my AI-powered vacuum cleaner, may you one day take over the world—WL

PENGUIN WORKSHOP
An imprint of Penguin Random House LLC
1745 Broadway, New York, NY 10019
penguinrandomhouse.com

Library of Congress Cataloging-in-Publication Data is available.

First published in the United States of America by Penguin Workshop, 2026

Manufactured in the United States of America
CJKW

ISBN 9798217050963 (paperback)
10 9 8 7 6 5 4 3 2 1

ISBN 9798217050970 (library binding)
10 9 8 7 6 5 4 3 2 1

The authorized representative in the EU for product safety and compliance is Penguin Random House Ireland, Morrison Chambers, 32 Nassau Street, Dublin D02 YH68, Ireland, https://eu-contact.penguin.ie.

Contents

What Is AI?

For more than seventy years, making computers that are smarter than humans has been the goal of some computer scientists (people who build and program computers). Since the creation of computers in the 1950s, scientists have fantasized about the possibilities of artificial intelligence, or AI. AI is a tool that helps computers to identify patterns, solve problems, and perform tasks by analyzing data.

As computers have become more powerful, AI is now a part of our everyday lives. Once, we picked up a telephone and made a call to a restaurant. People now type with AI to learn how soon their online order will be delivered. There was a time when we wrote down reminders and appointments, but now we ask a digital assistant, such as Siri or Alexa, to add them to our calendars. And we once relied on paper maps. But now AI shows and tells us turn-by-turn directions to work or school.

The goal of artificial intelligence is efficiency. A computer program can analyze a process and decide the fastest way to complete a task or chore.

Though the term "artificial intelligence" might sound like movie magic, AI is simply computer programs designed by humans that follow a set of directions that have been created by a computer engineer or software developer.

This isn't a new idea. In fact, every video game we play, every website we visit, and every phone app we download are just computer programs that follow the directions of the person who made them.

But there are big differences between video games and AI. A video game recognizes only the data it has been given. Meanwhile, AI can handle large amounts of information, rapidly analyze it, and make a quick decision on how to react to what it "sees." How AI interprets that information is what makes it an "intelligence."

In the last forty years alone, AI has become more powerful than ever. But with each passing year, AI becomes stronger, faster, and smarter. The long-term goal for many computer scientists is to create AI systems that have the same intellectual abilities as humans . . . or beyond.

CHAPTER 1
The Birth of Artificial Intelligence

Before humans could invent AI, someone first had to invent the computer. That person was Charles Babbage, a mathematician living in London, England.

In 1812, Charles cofounded a group called the Analytical Society. The group researched many of the best mathematical techniques from around the world and taught them to students and scientists in England. It was during this time that the idea for calculating numbers using a machine came to Charles.

Charles Babbage

In the 1820s and 1830s, Charles created the difference engine. This large metal device showed the numbers zero through nine on metal wheels. When one of the wheels turned from nine back to zero, the next wheel advanced by one. The difference engine was better than other calculators of the time, as it worked with up to twenty digits at once.

The difference engine

Charles's next invention, the analytical engine, was made up of four parts: the mill, the store, the reader, and the printer. Believe it or not, this analytical engine shared similar parts with present-day computers. The "mill" was like a processor, where information is calculated. The "store" was storage space. The "reader" was equal to a screen to visualize information. The "printer" was an output, similar to a printer we might have at home. This was an early type of computer that was designed to be programmed using "punch cards" that contained data.

Charles worked on his analytical engine until his death in 1871. He became known as the Father of the Computer, even though he didn't live long enough to build the machine he designed.

The next major advancement in the computer also came from London. The mathematician Alan Turing was born in 1912. Alan was a curious young man who enjoyed solving puzzles and math problems. In college, Alan studied mathematics and probability theory, the possibilities of something happening. In 1936, while attempting to solve a very difficult math equation, Alan came up with the Turing machine. Unlike Charles Babbage's analytical engine, Alan's invention was not a machine but an idea. Alan believed that any equation could be solved by following a set of written instructions, or a process. Charles Babbage may have been the Father of the Computer, but Alan Turing became the Father of the Computer Program.

Alan Turing

By 1938, Alan joined the Government Code and Cypher School, but his studies were cut short when World War II broke out the next year. Alan's role in the war was to decode transmissions intercepted from the German Army. This was an ideal match for a young man who enjoyed solving puzzles. During his time in the military, Alan designed several code-breaking machines, including two called

Bombe and Tunny, which decoded more than eighty-four thousand enemy messages every month.

The analytical engine and the Turing machine were amazing ideas, but they only performed single tasks. They solved math equations in specific ways.

The Government Code and Cypher School

At the start of World War I, the United Kingdom created two military organizations to find and decode communications sent by the German Army. Understanding these messages helped to stop attacks by enemy planes and ships.

In 1919, these two organizations merged to form the Government Code and Cypher School, which continued to play an important role during World War II, intercepting thousands of enemy messages, breaking the German Enigma codes, and saving countless lives.

In 1946, a year after World War II ended, the organization was renamed the Government Communications Headquarters (GCHQ), which it is still called today.

While World War II raged on, a German engineer named Konrad Zuse was hidden away in a laboratory in Berlin. Konrad had gone from making calculators to creating the first programmable computer, which he called the Z3. The invention was important, because for the first time, a computer performed more than one task. The Z3 could add, subtract, multiply, divide, and calculate square roots.

Konrad Zuse

The Z3 looked nothing like the computers we have today. It had no screen, and it was so large, it took up an entire room! The computer was programmed by inserting punch cards with instructions into the device. The Z3 read the cards and performed the requested action.

Z3

While Konrad Zuse's computer was far from the laptops and tablets of today, the Z3's ability to perform multiple actions was innovative. Many scientists were determined to improve on the idea.

Frederic Williams and Tom Kilburn with the Manchester Baby

The next people to do exactly that were British computer scientists Frederic Williams and Tom Kilburn. The men worked together at the University of Manchester, in England. Using the Z3 as inspiration, they designed and built their own computer in 1948, known as the Manchester Baby.

Like the Z3, the Manchester Baby took up a whole room and weighed almost one ton.

The Baby improved on the Z3 by having multiple programs for calculating numbers already built in. Computers today can play games, do math, and process words, all because of the Manchester Baby's creative design.

Alan Turing remained a leader in developing computers. He created math-solving programs for both the Manchester Baby and the Ferranti Mark 1. The Ferranti, an updated version of the Manchester Baby, used digital elements and so was smaller in size.

Alan saw little difference between a computer and the human brain. He was fascinated by the idea that humans might one day "talk" to computers. This was the beginning of artificial intelligence, although it didn't yet have an official name. He wondered: If humans and computers *did* communicate with each other, how would we tell them apart? This was the question that sparked Alan's next creation, the Turing test.

Proposed in 1950, the Turing test was created to see if humans could tell the difference between machine intelligence and human intelligence.

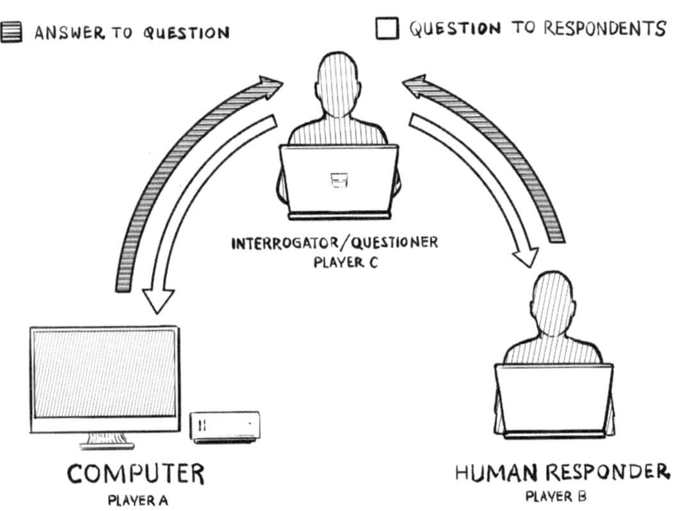

Alan asked people to sit at a computer and type questions. On the other end was either a human or a computer that answered back. If the person could correctly tell when they were speaking to a computer, the computer would "fail" the test.

As scientists today work to create AI that can hold full conversations, the Turing test remains an important step. With each passing year, more AI programs are mistaken for being human, and it's only a matter of time before we cannot tell the difference at all.

CHAPTER 2
The Golden Age

By 1950, all the key components for computers as we know them had been created. By 1951, fully built computers were available to the public, advertised as "electronic brains."

Early computers were too large to fit on desks, or inside homes, so they were mostly purchased by government offices, banks, and universities. In the United States, the UNIVAC I was the first computer available for sale.

The UNIVAC I was eight feet tall, fourteen feet wide, and weighed nearly thirty thousand pounds! The UNIVAC I wasn't made for fun. It couldn't play games. And the internet wouldn't be invented until 1983. All these early computers did was process and calculate numbers.

UNIVAC I

For many businesses, including insurance companies and the United States Census Bureau, that's exactly what they needed.

As computers became the next big thing, people wanted to learn how to use or create them. Alan Turing had published the idea for his Turing test in a scientific journal called *MIND* in 1950. Scientists who read the article were excited by the idea of talking to computers. Suddenly, many of them were thinking about AI, and an even smaller group set out to create it!

One person who was very interested in the possibilities of AI was a computer scientist named John McCarthy. While teaching math at Dartmouth College in New Hampshire, John invited scientists from across the country to visit Dartmouth and share ideas. In his invitation, John used the term "artificial intelligence" for the first time as the topic for the meeting. The name stuck.

John McCarthy

During John's meeting, participants discussed how they could produce intelligent responses from a computer. They wondered: How could computers be "smart" if they were following sets of instructions (called algorithms) to complete a task?

While these scientists had big dreams, computers were still new. Their technological components weren't nearly as powerful as those we have today. John and his friends left the meeting excited by the possibilities of AI. First, however, they had to build it.

Software, or directions that tell a computer what to do, is created with programming languages. These are the instructions the computer follows. Since a programming language for AI didn't yet exist, John McCarthy created one in 1958 called LISP (which stands for "list processing"). LISP was the first language of its kind and is still used in AI programming.

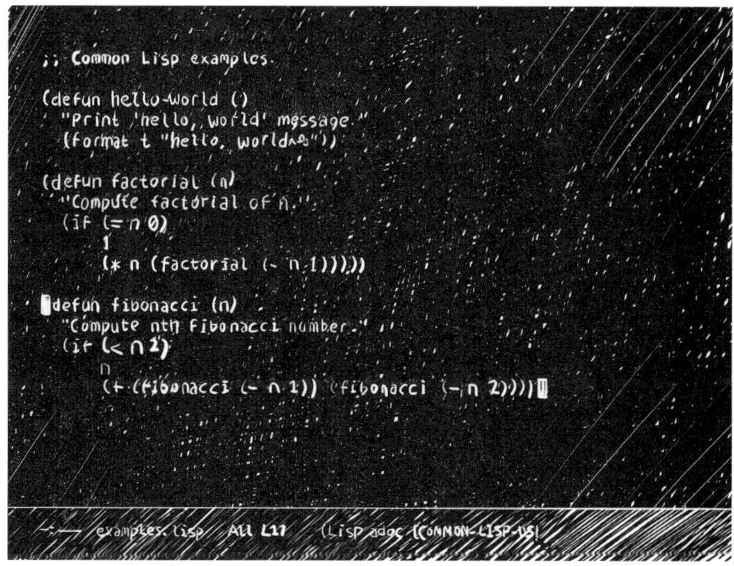

John's meeting at Dartmouth kicked off what became known as the Golden Age of AI, which lasted from 1956 to 1974. More advancement in AI happened over those two decades than in all prior history. John became an authority on AI and went on to teach at Stanford University, near San Francisco, California. In 1963, he founded the Stanford Artificial Intelligence Lab, a place for scientists interested in AI to research, test, explore, and create.

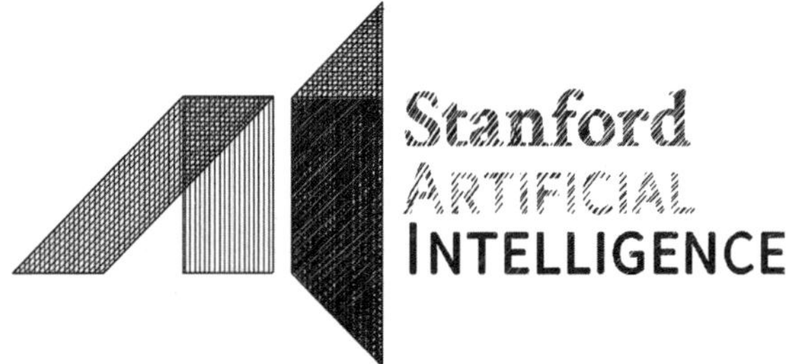

The lab at Stanford brought many brilliant students to California. By 1971, the area around Stanford came to be called Silicon Valley. Silicon is a powerful element used to create many of the electronic parts found inside computers.

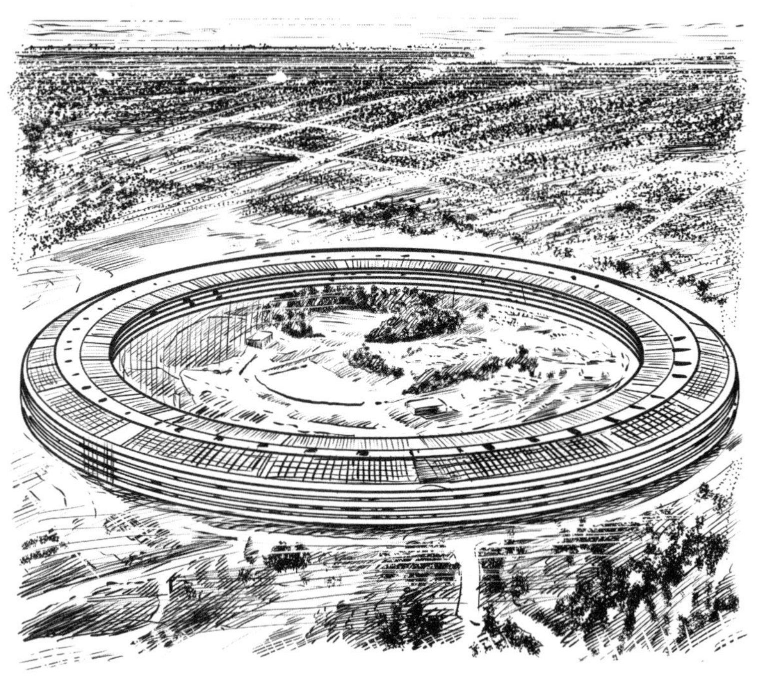

Apple headquarters in Silicon Valley

Silicon Valley became the most important place to be for people wanting to work in technology. To this day, it's home to corporations such as Apple, Meta, Google, and others.

John McCarthy realized that making a computer that would be as smart as a human was no easy task. Rather than build it all at once, he split researchers into teams. Each team focused on what they saw as the most important aspects of AI.

One team developed a system to give AI perception, allowing the computer to understand information that came from sensors, cameras, or microphones. Another team focused on machine learning, allowing a computer to make decisions based on the information it was given. Yet another attempted to build a system for natural language processing, or the ability for a computer to "read" information. Other teams focused on problem-solving and reasoning. It was John's hope that, once each system was perfected, they could be brought together to create a humanlike mind.

Unfortunately, the AI systems John wanted to create were impossible at the time. Computers were not yet powerful enough to perform such difficult functions.

ARTIFICIAL INTELLIGENCE LABORATORY

During this time, the public had heard tales about the wonders of artificial intelligence. Newspapers were filled with stories of all the amazing, futuristic things that computers would soon do. Scientists like John had made promises they couldn't keep. The excitement of the public turned to disbelief and frustration.

By 1974, an AI Winter—a time where little progress was made—had set in. But by 1980, AI research went from being a small section of computing to being one of the most exciting areas of science.

CHAPTER 3
Types of AI

Just as computers come in all shapes and sizes, so does artificial intelligence. Scientists file AI programs into one of three categories. How the programs are sorted depends on their function.

The first type is known as narrow AI. These programs are the most basic and perform only one main function. A common example of narrow AI is a robot vacuum cleaner. These robots are programmed for one purpose: to clean our floors.

While they can recognize the space around them (so they can move around walls, pets, or people), their navigational skills exist to support their cleaning function.

Another example of narrow AI is a computer program made to play chess against a human opponent. After a human makes a move, the narrow AI responds with its own.

A third example of narrow AI can be found in our email. Every email inbox comes with something called a spam filter. (Spam emails are those that are unrequested and unexpected, similar to junk mail that shows up in your physical mailbox.) This narrow AI looks at each incoming message and decides

if it's coming from a familiar or approved sender. If it is, the AI passes it to our inbox. If not, the message goes to the spam folder.

But sometimes these systems get things wrong. An AI-powered vacuum cleaner may skip over a dirty spot on the floor. An AI chess player may make a silly move and lose the game. An AI email filter may accidentally send an important email to spam. Narrow AI programs will never get better at what they do, because they cannot learn.

The second type of AI is general AI. These systems are smarter than narrow AI because they *can* learn.

You may have heard of Siri and Alexa. These systems are known as digital assistants. They answer basic questions, set reminders, and can help us make phone calls. When you ask Siri to search the internet, or tell Alexa to play a song, general AI must first recognize the voice, then interpret the words, and, finally, decide what to do next.

Another example of general AI is a chatbot, which you may have seen if you or your parents ever go on a website to look for help. These "bots" are trained to recognize keywords in text and respond with the best possible answer to our questions.

General AI analyzes information and responds through speech, text, or actions. General AI programs like Siri, Alexa, and chatbots make mistakes from time to time, but they "learn" from their mistakes and change the way they respond in the future. The more a general AI is used over time, the stronger, or "smarter," it becomes.

The ability of AI to reach the correct conclusion without specific directions is known as "machine learning." To learn, AI looks for patterns or repetitions in information. If we ask Alexa to play a song and it plays the wrong one, we'll likely tell it to stop and try again. Alexa's programming notes how we say the song name to help recognize it again in the future. The software inside a tablet can translate our scratchy handwriting into typed text. The more of a specific handwriting the AI analyzes, the better the translation will become.

There is even a general AI that used machine learning to play video games! In 2015, a group of scientists attached an Atari 2600, a video game console released in 1977, to a computer program. The AI, called DeepMind, could access forty-nine Atari games, but was given no instructions on how to play them. DeepMind spent weeks playing the games over and over. It learned from its mistakes until it had mastered twenty-nine of the games. (Its favorite game was *Breakout*.)

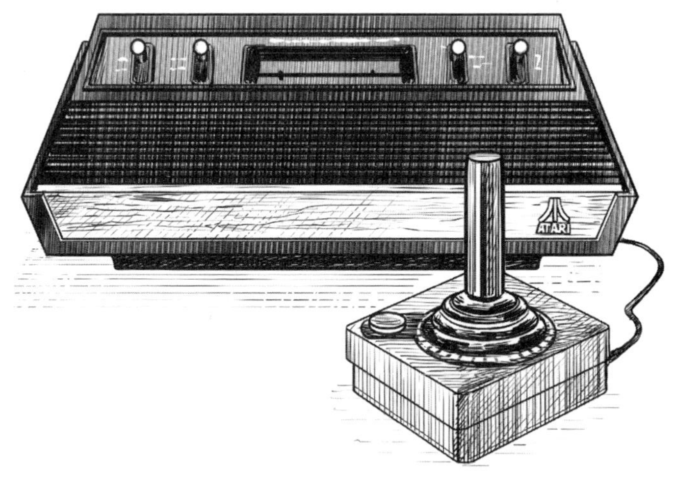

Atari 2600

To make it easier for AI to learn, scientists developed "neural networks." These complicated structures imitate a system that has already shown that it can learn new information quickly: the human brain.

Neurons are cells in our brains that transmit information. Our brains contain around one hundred billion neurons, and each one has more than ten thousand connections. When these neurons "fire" (send a signal), our brains retrieve needed information, such as an address or a memory.

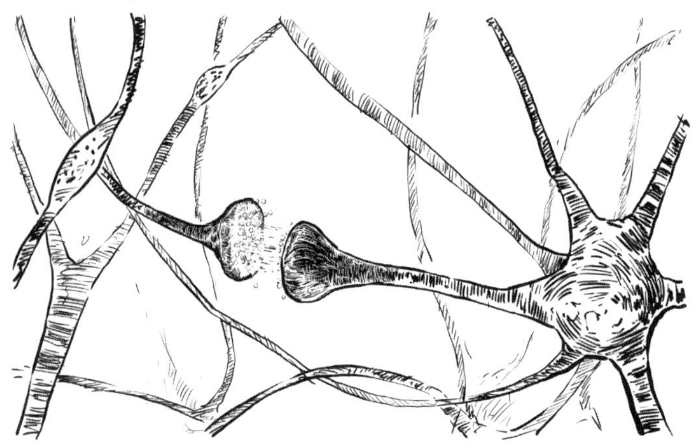

Neurons firing in the human brain

The idea for neural networks was first proposed in the 1940s. It wasn't until the 1990s that scientists were able to simulate a brain with roughly one hundred neurons. By 2016, technology had improved so much that scientists could simulate electronic brains with one million neurons.

The success of machine learning and neural networks leads us into the final type of AI, called super AI.

Working with a super AI is like interacting with a person who is a genius. They can answer *any* question or solve *any* math problem someone could possibly come up with! Super AI might even find solutions to the biggest problems affecting our world. They might tell us how to fix climate change, end pollution, or even invent cures for diseases. Super AI could do all these things . . . if it existed.

Right now, super AI is only a theory, or an

idea. It doesn't exist because computers are not yet powerful enough to create it. But even if we could build a super AI, does that mean we should? Super AI might help to solve problems by providing new and creative solutions, but it could just as easily spread false information and cause even bigger problems.

Super AI is exactly what Charles Babbage, Alan Turing, and John McCarthy thought of when they dreamed about the future of computers. And yet, almost one hundred years later, we still cannot achieve it. But that hasn't stopped computer scientists from trying.

CHAPTER 4
Breaking New Ground

The first age of AI lasted from 1956 until 1974. Scientists were eager to prove that computers could do all kinds of amazing things. Early attempts at AI may seem simple compared to today's technology, but they were great achievements of their time.

One of the first AI systems was called ELIZA. It was developed in 1966 by Joseph Weizenbaum, a computer scientist at the Massachusetts Institute of Technology (also known as MIT), in Cambridge, Massachusetts.

Joseph Weizenbaum

ELIZA was created to be the first computerized psychotherapist—a machine that could diagnose and treat mental health and behavioral disorders. This narrow AI asked users how they were feeling. Based on a user's typed response, ELIZA asked questions or offered advice. It was the first AI that could "talk" with humans. However, ELIZA wasn't truly communicating with anyone. Just like some chatbots do, it followed a pre-written script.

The software that powered ELIZA was an early natural language processing program. This means that it looked for patterns in words and sentences. If a user told ELIZA that they were feeling sad, the software provided a standard "sad" response. Even though ELIZA was limited in what it could do, many people felt better after typing with it.

ELIZA is responsible for something known as the ELIZA effect. This occurs when people falsely believe that an AI feels emotions or is more intelligent than it truly is. Artificial intelligence can't understand humans. It only imitates understanding.

When most people think about AI, they think of robots. While an AI doesn't *have* to be contained within a robot, another early attempt was.

Shakey the Robot was created by scientists at the Stanford Research Institute in 1966. Shakey was little more than a computer on wheels with a camera mounted on top, but what made the robot impressive was its camera's ability to see its surroundings. Scientists sent Shakey commands

using a computer. Shakey then performed the action. It located large boxes and pushed them to another location. If Shakey encountered obstacles, it used reasoning to move around them. However, it took Shakey as long as fifteen minutes to analyze and complete scientists' instructions.

Shakey was limited in its abilities but was groundbreaking in proving that an AI could be made to move on its own.

The scientists responsible for Shakey formed a new company called SRI International. SRI made important contributions to the world of technology, including inkjet printing and liquid crystal displays (LCD). In 2010, the company released its most important piece of technology: a mobile app known as Siri.

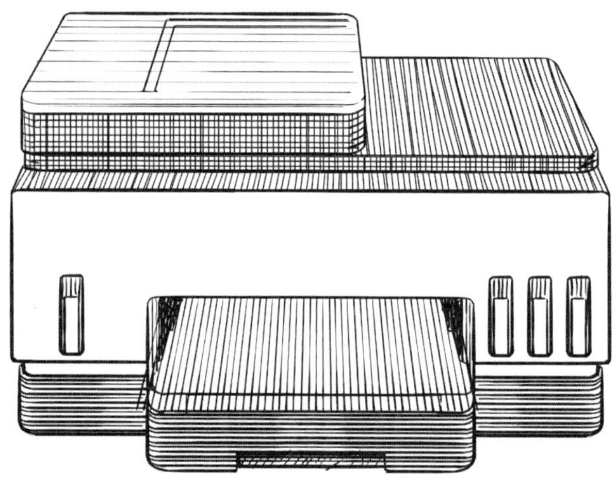

Mathematician and computer scientist Alan Turing

Seuddeutsche Zeitung Photo/Alamy

The first programmable computer, the Z3, created in 1941

Jeff Morris/PA Images/Getty Images

Computer scientists Tom Kilburn and Frederic Williams with the Manchester Baby computer

H. Armstrong Roberts/ClassicStock/Archive Photos/Getty Images

A data processing room with the UNIVAC I,
the first computer for sale in the United States, 1950s

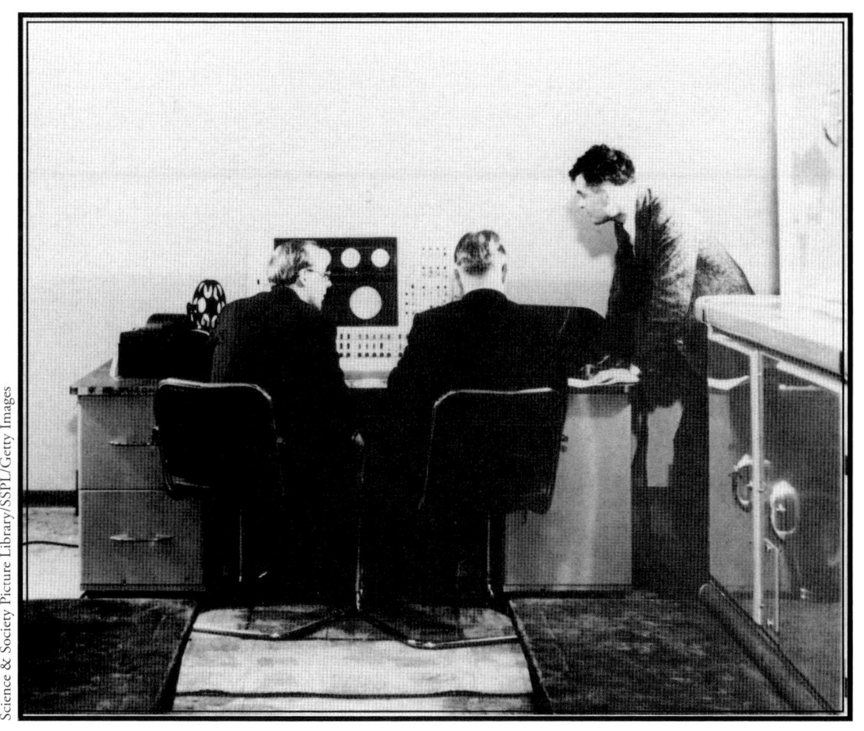

The Ferranti Mark 1 computer, created in 1951

Smith Archive/Alamy

Computer scientist and founder of the Stanford Artificial Intelligence Lab (SAIL), John McCarthy, 1966

Inventor of the ELIZA chatbot, Joseph Weizenbaum

World chess champion Garry Kasparov loses to
IBM's Deep Blue AI system, 1997

AI researcher Doug Lenat

Vaughn Youtz/ZUMA Press/Alamy

The driverless robotic vehicle Stanley wins the DARPA race, 2005

AI program Watson wins *Jeopardy!*, 2011

Karen Bleier/AFP/Getty Images

Siri debuts in the iPhone 4s, 2011

Bill Pugliano/Getty Images News/Getty Images

Tesla's Model S with autopilot self-driving features

Google's AlphaGo AI preparing to defeat a professional Go player

Wolfgang Kumm/picture alliance/Getty Images

Human Rights Watch protesting the use of
AI-powered autonomous weapons, 2019

Gregg Newton/AFP/Getty Images

A replica of NASA's Perseverance rover,
operated with the help of AI, 2020

Zhu Haipeng/VCG/Visual China Group/Getty Images

AI-programmed assembly line

Siri was created to help people interact with their phones using their voice. When users tell Siri what they want to do, the program follows the commands. Siri can launch phone calls, play music, create reminders, and search the internet.

Even in the earliest days of AI, scientists believed it could find its way into our everyday lives. Especially in applications of health care.

MYCIN was created at Stanford in 1972 by Bruce Buchanan and Ted Shortliffe. This AI was designed to be a doctor's assistant. It analyzed blood samples and identified possible diseases.

Bruce Buchanan

Ted Shortliffe

MYCIN was known as an expert system AI. This means the program imitated the decision-making abilities of a human expert. After examining blood samples, MYCIN could then suggest additional laboratory tests, or offer a diagnosis and treatment plan. The system was incorporated into medical trials in 1979.

Scientists believed that its results were as accurate as decisions made by medical experts.

Even with MYCIN's success, doctors were skeptical about using these computers in health care. If an AI made a mistake—making an incorrect diagnosis or missing important information—it would lead to problems for hospitals, doctors, and patients.

Though many systems created during the first age of AI accomplished amazing things, not every program met its goals.

While Shakey was pushing boxes around and MYCIN was examining blood samples, AI researcher Doug Lenat wanted to accomplish the impossible. He dreamed of building an AI that had a general knowledge of math, history, science, and literature.

Doug Lenat

Doug began work on the Cyc Project in 1984, but he quickly discovered why no one had created such a powerful AI. For a program to have so much "everyday knowledge," the information first needed to be programmed into a system. It would take two hundred years' worth of work to program all the data! After working on Cyc for more than ten years, Doug abandoned his dream. He knew that the Cyc Project might be impossible to create . . . and it was.

CHAPTER 5
A Show of Spectacle

The systems created during the first age of AI mostly interested other scientists. Outside of laboratories and conferences, the average person didn't understand or have access to artificial intelligence.

During the second age of AI, from 1996 to the present day, scientists wanted to dazzle the public with their creations. Scientists knew that to bring awareness to the possibilities of AI, they needed to get people talking about it and having fun with it.

Before the DeepMind AI played Atari video games all by itself, an earlier version mastered chess.

Deep Thought was created in 1985 at Carnegie

Mellon University by scientists Murray Campbell, Feng-hsiung Hsu, and Thomas Anantharaman. The chess-playing AI ran on a series of algorithms (patterns) that analyzed its opponent's moves and responded accordingly. By 1988, Deep Thought had proven its skill by defeating chess grandmaster Bent Larsen.

Feng-hsiung Hsu and Murray Campbell winning a prize for Deep Thought's chess performance

Electronics research company IBM heard about Deep Thought and realized they could create an exciting event for the public. IBM hired Campbell, Hsu, and Anantharaman in 1989 to create a chess-playing AI that could defeat a world champion.

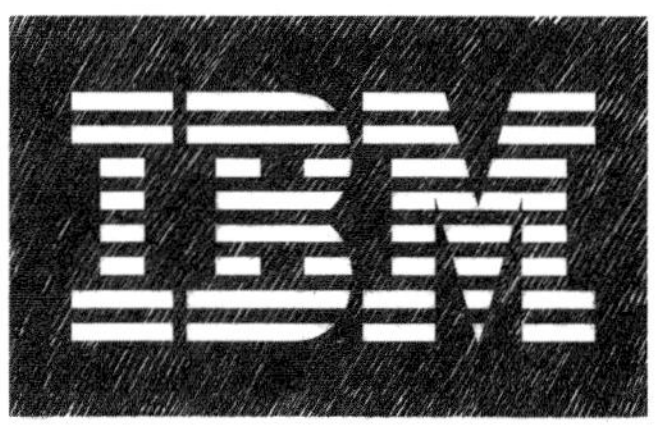

This new AI, called Deep Blue, was not just programmed to respond, but to think one step ahead. Deep Blue considered all the moves a chess opponent might make. It also analyzed the possible success rate of each move. The main struggle its creators had to overcome was time. They didn't want Deep Blue to take fifteen minutes between moves. They wanted it to respond quickly to make for an exciting game. To shorten Deep Blue's thinking time, IBM created new, faster circuits (paths for conducting electric current).

After seven years, in 1996, Deep Blue was ready to take on the best chess player in the world. During an event held in Philadelphia, Pennsylvania, Russian chess master Garry Kasparov sat down with Deep Blue for six games. Scientists at IBM had high hopes for their AI. They were stunned when the chess master defeated Deep Blue three times.

After some updates to the system, Deep Blue and Garry Kasparov played again the following year. This time, Deep Blue defeated the chess master twice. Three more games ended in a tie. The event made the national news, and viewers considered how this "man versus machine" matchup might impact the development of future technology.

Meanwhile, Shakey's creator, SRI International, influenced technology in its own way. After Siri, SRI's digital personal assistant, was released, Apple purchased the AI for more than $200 million.

ACM Chess Challenge
Garry Kasparov
VS
DEEP BLUE
Garry
Kasparov
DEEP BLUE
acm

Siri was added to every new iPhone by 2011. Suddenly, everyone could have an AI in their pocket. Now iPhone users could make calls, compose emails, or set appointments by speaking into their phones and giving Siri voice commands.

While digital assistants are commonplace now, Siri's technology was ahead of its time. Microsoft's AI assistant Cortana and Amazon's

Alexa didn't become available until 2014. These AI systems operate through natural language processing and speech recognition. The more we use them, the better they become at understanding our commands.

Voice-controlled AI is fun, but it isn't perfect. Currently, it operates with only 95 percent accuracy. Scientists believe that once voice-controlled AI reaches 99 percent accuracy, speech will become the main way that humans interact with computers.

Following Deep Blue's chess win, IBM wanted to wow people again. The company revealed a powerful new natural language processing AI named Watson, which could answer nearly any knowledge-based question it was asked. It took a team of twenty scientists more than five years to build Watson. To test Watson's abilities, IBM took its AI to a place where intelligence mattered—the TV quiz game show *Jeopardy!*

In February 2011, Watson competed on *Jeopardy!* against Ken Jennings and Brad Rutter. These were the contestants who had won the most matches and the most amount of

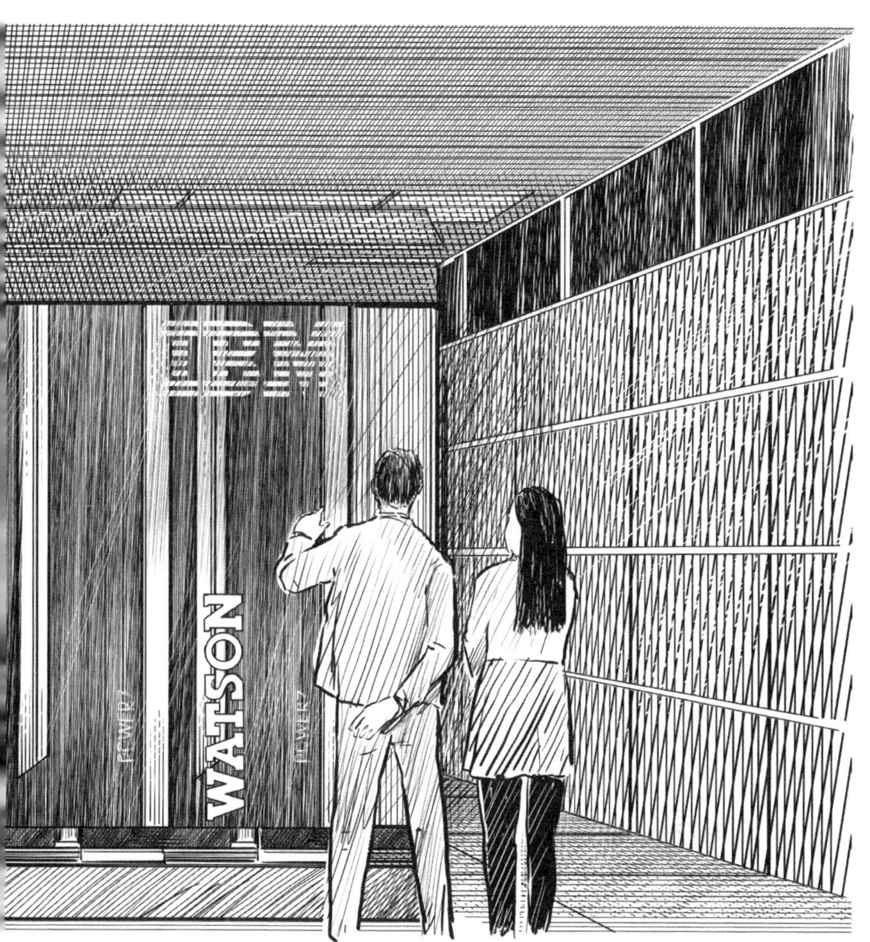

money in the show's history. During the two-day televised event—watched by more than thirty million people—Watson defeated both opponents.

How AI Won at *Jeopardy!*

To prepare for the 2011 *Jeopardy!* game, IBM's Watson AI first competed against one hundred former *Jeopardy!* winners. Then, scientists uploaded two hundred million pages of information to Watson's servers, which were stored backstage. To keep the match as fair as possible, Watson was not allowed to connect to the internet. Watson received the game clues in writing at the same time Ken Jennings and Brad Rutter heard them.

Although the AI had to read the questions, interpret them, search its servers for information, decide on an answer, and ring in before its opponents, its speed and processing power couldn't be matched by the two humans it was playing against.

$77,147
Who Is Bram
Stoker?
$ 17,973

AI had proven it was more than just a flashy gimmick. It was doing things that an average human couldn't. Many technology companies paid large sums of money to purchase AI research businesses, or created their own. After DeepMind learned to play Atari games, Google purchased the technology in 2014 for more than $400 million.

Two years later, DeepMind returned with another showy display for the public. Its new AI, called AlphaGo, played the traditional Chinese board game Go at a professional level. Go is considered to be the most difficult board game to master. During testing, AlphaGo defeated European Go champion Fan Hui in a private event. But Google wanted to show the entire world what its AI could do.

Months later, AlphaGo competed against world champion Lee Sedol during a match held in Seoul, South Korea. AlphaGo won the contest, four games to one. The event was filmed and released in 2017 as a Netflix documentary called *AlphaGo*. The same year, AlphaGo took on the world's highest-ranked player, Ke Jie of China. AlphaGo won all three games against its skilled opponent.

Go

Go is a board game believed to have been invented more than four thousand years ago in China, and remains popular today in China, South Korea, and Japan.

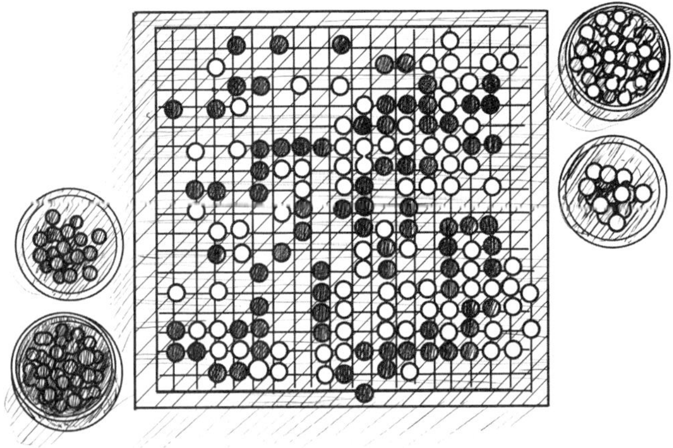

It is played on a wooden board showing a grid nineteen tiles high and nineteen tiles wide. The game uses flat white and black pieces called stones. At each turn, stones are placed at intersections on the board. The goal of the game is to claim as much territory, or board space, as possible. At the end of the game, the player with the largest amount of territory and greatest number of captured stones is the winner.

Winning Go requires critical thinking, skill, and strategy. Part of the game's appeal is its variety, since no two games are alike. While Go may sound complex, the rules are so simple that it is suitable for all ages.

In 2019, AI made its first appearance in the world of esports, or professional gaming. A system called OpenAI had learned to play *Dota 2*, a five-versus-five multiplayer game, by studying professional players. Using neural networks, OpenAI had gone from new player to master in record time. OpenAI defeated the world

championship team, OG, in two out of three games.

Suddenly, it appeared that the machines had the ability to surpass humans. While playing board games and video games entertained the public, scientists knew there were even more applications for AI in our everyday lives.

CHAPTER 6
Science Fact or Fiction?

Although AI can do incredible things, scientists are always looking to push technology further. As this happens, our everyday world begins looking more and more like science fiction (stories that are based on imagined technology, time travel, and other scientific advances).

Today, more AI systems are being designed to run autonomously (say: ah-TAHN-oh-MUSS-ly), or without direct control by humans. But if autonomous AI is so powerful, why aren't our roads filled with driverless vehicles? Because the technology has not yet been perfected.

Driving a car is difficult. Licensed drivers must understand the rules of driving, traffic patterns, and how a car works. They need to know when to accelerate, when to brake, when to use a turn signal, and what all the road signs mean. Drivers must also be able to react safely when other drivers *don't* follow the rules of the road. A split-second decision can be the difference between getting into an accident or avoiding it entirely. Each year, there are more than one million traffic-related deaths around the world. In the future, driverless cars could make transportation safer for us all.

If a driverless car were the only vehicle on a road, it would work very well. The presence of other vehicles is what makes perfecting this technology so difficult. An autonomous vehicle needs perception, or the ability to "see" and react to obstacles such as other cars, people, or even junk on the roadway.

Autonomous vehicles were predicted as early as 1940, when a drawing of a driverless car appeared in an issue of the magazine *Popular Science*.

In that issue, scientists predicted that cars would be driving themselves as soon as 1975. Nearly ninety years later, they still are not commonplace.

A European research organization called Eureka launched the Prometheus Project in 1986. The goal of the program was to create the first self-driving car. In 1995, scientists almost succeeded. After filling a large van with electronics, radio equipment, and four cameras (for perception), the driverless vehicle traveled more than one thousand miles from Munich, Germany, to Copenhagen, Denmark, and back again. The van reached speeds of more than one hundred miles per hour and shared the roadway with actual drivers. However, the van rarely traveled more than one hundred miles before it had to stop and allow scientists to make adjustments.

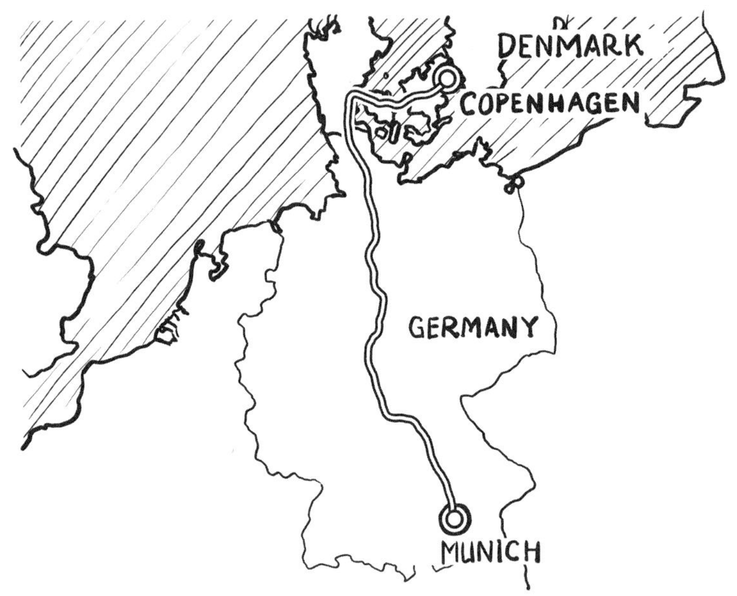

Almost ten years later, the United States launched its own research into autonomous vehicles through the Defense Advanced Research Projects Agency (also known as DARPA). This US government agency is responsible for developing new technologies for national security. Researchers were invited to design self-driving vehicles that could travel more than 150 miles without any assistance from humans. The first Grand Challenge was held in 2004. There was a $1 million prize for the team whose vehicle could travel the fastest from Barstow, California, to Primm, Nevada. Out of more than one hundred teams, none of the vehicles succeeded.

The next year, DARPA's Grand Challenge featured a $2 million prize. This time, nearly two hundred teams raced their driverless vehicles across the desert. Five teams completed the challenge. The winning vehicle, called Stanley, was designed at Stanford University.

Since then, automobile companies have invested a lot of money to bring the first self-driving cars to the public. Two companies focused on this technology are Tesla Motors and Waymo. While Waymo focused on creating self-driving taxis, Tesla included an "autopilot" mode in its Model S electric cars in 2014.

Tesla's Model S

The autopilot function controls acceleration, braking, and steering, but the vehicle requires its driver to remain alert in the event of an emergency.

As technology improves, Tesla's autopilot features will grow. Soon, drivers will be able to step out of their vehicle at a destination, and the car will park itself safely in a nearby lot. When it's time to leave, the vehicle will be summoned by tapping a button on a smartphone, starting the car and then instructing it to move to its driver's location.

Science fiction is beginning to sound a lot like science fact.

CHAPTER 7
Generating Creativity

While it may sound like artificial intelligence is something that only scientists can use in a laboratory, that couldn't be further from the truth. Anyone with a computer, tablet, or smartphone can use artificial intelligence!

Generative AI—artificial intelligence that creates (or "generates") images, words, music, and videos—is available to everyone. Generative AI gained popularity in 2018 when a computer manufacturing company created an AI that showed realistic photos of humans. The most interesting part was that none of the people in the photos existed!

Two types of popular generative AI are called ChatGPT and DALL-E. Both systems work through user prompts. A person inputs text (words), and the AI creates a response. Users can ask ChatGPT to tell them about anything—an animal, a movie, or a fun fact about our solar system—and the system provides a short answer that appears as if it was written by a person. But AI can produce wrong answers because it doesn't have the ability to fact-check itself. That's why it's important to confirm information with reliable sources.

Every day, more people use generative AI to help them work efficiently. For example,

ChatGPT can translate text into other languages, brainstorm a list of ideas, and even help write an email or text message.

ChatGPT can also act as a tutor, helping someone to understand difficult math equations or learn a new language. It can plan a workout for anyone looking to build strength. You can even tell ChatGPT what you have in your refrigerator, and it will suggest recipes that you can make for dinner from those ingredients.

In 2024, Apple added ChatGPT to its phones. Named Apple Intelligence, the AI learns how users interact with their phones and makes processes more efficient. Apple Intelligence can instantly transcribe spoken conversations to text, summarize an email or website article, and create an emoji that's never been seen before!

Apple Intelligence

But generative AI can be used for fun, too. Some people use ChatGPT to help them write stories. However, ChatGPT is not intended to be used by children under the age of thirteen.

OpenAI, the same research lab responsible for ChatGPT, also created DALL-E. Named after Spanish artist Salvador Dalí and the fictional robot from the Pixar film *WALL-E*, this generative AI uses prompts to create works of art. A person can describe what they want to see, and DALL-E will create it (or something close to it) in a few seconds. Want to see an octopus playing a drum set? No problem! A futuristic city? Simple! A brand-new superhero? Just describe them!

Users can even ask DALL-E to create the image in the same style as a famous painter, like Vincent van Gogh, Frida Kahlo, or Dalí himself.

A DALL-E painting created in the style of Salvador Dalí

Some generative AI can write songs. Suno AI, developed in Cambridge, Massachusetts, writes music. Using Suno, anyone can create a hip-hop song about broccoli or a country song about doing math homework with just a few clicks.

While Suno can come up with both lyrics and music based on prompts for the song's subject and style, users can write their own lyrics and choose whether they'll be sung by a male or female "voice." Photos from a summer vacation can be uploaded to the service and Suno will create the perfect soundtrack to match them.

Many of these generative AI systems draw from existing written works or original works of art that are protected by copyright. Copyright grants an author or creator legal protection from unauthorized use. Because of this, people shouldn't sell what they create using ChatGPT and DALL-E.

While these tools can be a fun way to experiment with new types of art and unlock our creativity, new laws regarding AI-generated content are expected to protect work that is copyrighted by the original creators.

CHAPTER 8
Calculated Risks

Most computer scientists are focused on creating artificial intelligence systems that will make our lives easier or more efficient. Self-driving cars might make transportation safer. Machine learning systems will teach our electronic devices how to respond to our needs. Generative systems will help us create new types of art in the blink of an eye.

But some AI also has the potential to harm society.

At the 2024 World Economic Forum, leaders in business, politics, and education agreed that 40 percent of jobs were at risk of being replaced by AI in the near future. The careers that do remain will probably use AI to increase efficiency.

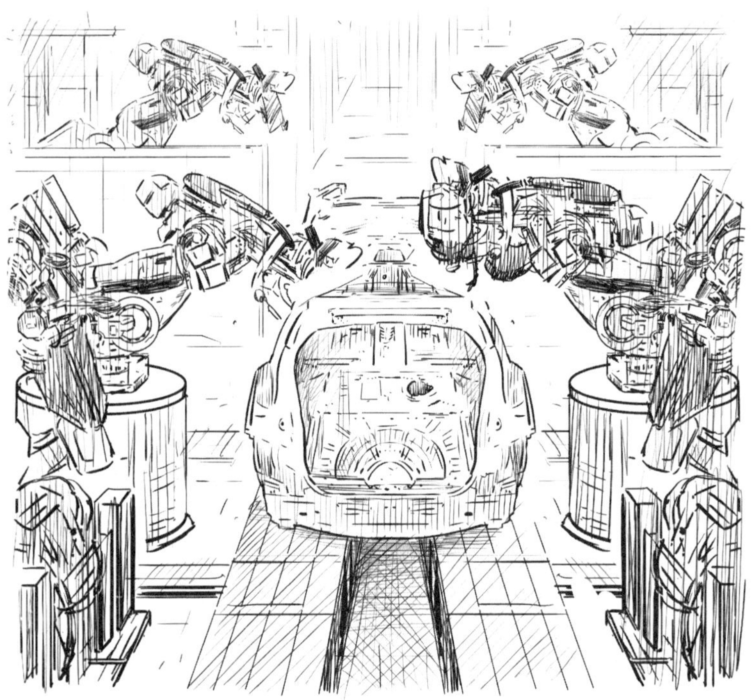

The jobs most likely to be lost to AI are those that analyze numbers and data. Factory jobs that can be automated by machines could also be lost. It might not sound like a bad idea to hand repetitive roles over to artificial intelligence systems. But it will take opportunities away from people who need jobs to meet their basic needs.

Another threat comes in the form of something called "deepfakes." Deepfakes are a type of generative AI that create images, video, or audio that portray something that doesn't actually exist. Some deepfakes can even generate realistic video of events that never occurred. In this way, AI can affect our ability to know what is real.

Imagine the problems that could be caused by a deepfake of a politician saying terrible things about another country, or their own. Celebrities can have their careers ruined by being deepfaked into offensive situations that never happened. Deepfakes can even open the door to bullying or mistrust among people around the world.

As AI takes on even larger roles in our lives, it's important that we don't believe everything we see and read. A news headline, a video, or even an audio clip may not be real. All these things are now easily generated by AI. It will become more and more important that we learn how to fact-check our news from multiple trusted sources to know what information we should truly believe.

Fake videos may be frightening, but it's AI-powered weapons that are truly terrifying.

Uncrewed, remotely controlled aircraft, called drones, have been used as military tools in various ways since the 1930s. Some can fly as high and as fast as fighter jets and drop missiles onto targets. But now militaries around the world are testing small, autonomous drones that carry weapons.

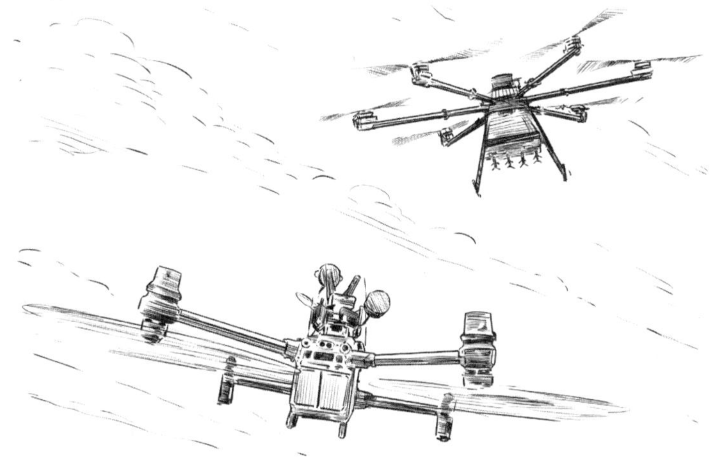

Because of their small size, these drones can be sent into buildings, caves, or forests that are too dangerous for people. Some of these drones can even make decisions about whether or not to act when they encounter enemy forces. The concern is that in the middle of a battle, drones could make incorrect decisions and hurt innocent people.

Current US laws require weaponized drones to be controlled by humans, but that could change in the future. Is it okay for an AI to decide whether to hurt someone? Computer programs don't understand the value of human life. If a drone makes a mistake, a situation could become even more dangerous. A drone meant to *stop* a war could just as easily *start* one.

Who takes the blame if a weaponized drone makes a poor decision? Do we blame the drone? The AI's creator? The programmers who built the software? When it comes to life-and-death situations, we must know who to hold responsible.

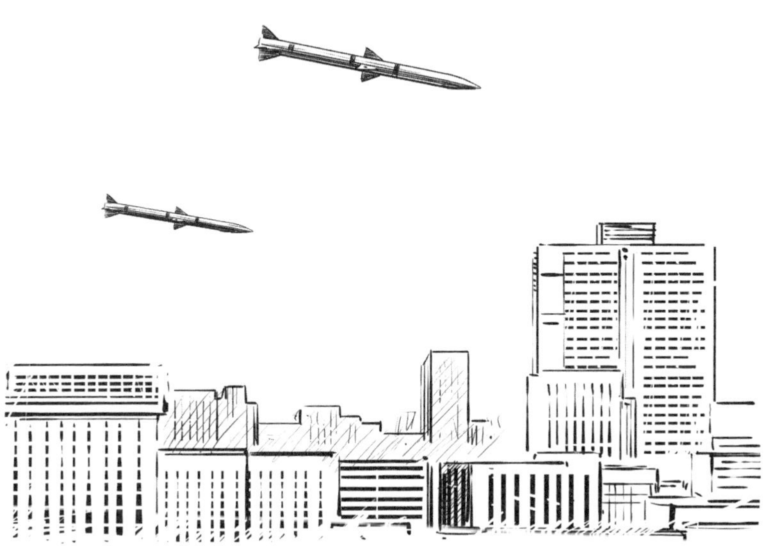

While we don't yet have the means to create super AI, many scientists are worried about the problems this technology might cause. The biggest threat from super AI is something called the "singularity."

An AI singularity might occur if artificial intelligence becomes smarter than people—representing a "singular" point in time where we can no longer predict the outcome of what AI can do. AI could create its own technology that we couldn't understand or control. This might cause significant changes to everything in our society. If humans can't understand the singularity's new technology, then we would be powerless to stop it.

There's no proof that the singularity will ever occur. But we must be aware of what challenges our planet might face as our technology grows and evolves to do more amazing things.

CHAPTER 9
Great Power, Greater Responsibility

Brilliant minds across the world are dreaming up new AI that will push the boundaries of what's possible. But does that mean they should?

Many scientists believe that AI should be created within a certain set of rules to prevent developing technology that might become dangerous. The idea of following a set of moral

standards that define right from wrong is known as "ethics."

While the ethics for artificial intelligence have not been fully defined, it hasn't stopped scientists from making suggestions and offering warnings.

Anytime new technologies are brought to consumers, there's the possibility that they can be weaponized by both civilians and militaries. In 2013, an organization known as Human Rights Watch launched a campaign called Stop Killer Robots. Its goal is to ban autonomous weapons systems.

In 2015, business leaders including Tesla CEO Elon Musk and Apple cofounder Steve Wozniak, as well as science experts like physicist Stephen Hawking, issued a public letter warning that AI could become more dangerous than nuclear weapons.

Steve Wozniak

Stephen Hawking, a brilliant scientist who studied the physics of black holes, believed that the creation of super AI could be the biggest event in the history of our civilization. But because of Stephen's fears regarding autonomous weaponized drones, he

Stephen Hawking

believed that without ethical standards, the invention of super AI might be humanity's last creation.

The ethics surrounding the use of AI came into the spotlight after police officers in Durham, England, put a general AI called the Harm Assessment Risk Tool (also known as HART) into use between 2016 and 2021.

After police arrested a suspect, HART looked at five years' worth of criminal data from the region to determine whether a person had a low, medium, or high risk of committing more crimes in the future. HART's recommendation was made by examining a suspect's background, age, and residential location.

The recommendations that HART gave were just suggestions. But the use of the HART AI raised several ethical questions. The final decision on whether a suspect was released or kept in custody needed to be made by a qualified officer.

But what if a police officer simply did whatever the AI recommended without trusting their own experience and knowledge?

The other issue that HART brought to light was something called "confirmation bias." This is when humans favor new information that confirms what they already believe. If a police officer felt that a suspect was dangerous, but lacked proof, the HART AI's recommendation might reinforce that officer's bias or prejudice. When a person forms opinions or feelings about someone because of their race, background, or religion without knowing them as an individual, that is prejudice. The situation becomes even more complicated when an AI is loaded with prejudiced information in the first place. If that is the case, an AI's decisions could never be fully trusted.

Even though official laws for creating AI don't yet exist, that doesn't mean the scientific community hasn't tried to create their own.

During the Asilomar Conference on Beneficial AI, held in California in 2017, experts agreed on twenty-three principles to guide future AI development. Most of the Asilomar Principles focused on ethics, safety, and ensuring that successful AI would benefit all humanity.

But these principles are not laws. AI researchers are free to develop new systems and tools without limit.

In March 2023, more than eighteen hundred technology leaders from Tesla, Microsoft, Apple, Amazon, DeepMind, Google, and Meta signed an open letter calling for a six-month pause on AI development.

In the letter, these professionals shared concerns that an AI more powerful than ChatGPT should only be developed once scientists were confident that the long-term effects would be positive ones. Unfortunately, the letter went ignored by most members of the AI community.

Months after the open letter was released, Microsoft cofounder Bill Gates issued a public statement on the risks of AI development. He worried that AI could negatively impact our world by spreading misinformation, creating bias, and damaging education. He encouraged scientists to develop AI in a responsible manner.

Bill Gates

Before the end of 2023, US president Joe Biden signed an executive order, or an official directive, relating to AI. The order ensured that the United States would lead the way in managing the risks of AI and set new standards for safety and security. The order included protections for privacy, innovation, and ensuring responsible AI use by the government.

There are also environmental impacts from AI that need to be addressed. AI requires enormous power and water resources, as well as land for the computers that produce it.

Only by creating and developing with ethics in mind can humans ensure that future AI is safe, secure, and trustworthy. A world of AI development without rules and moral standards might quickly become a dangerous one.

CHAPTER 10
The Future of AI

Twenty years ago, it would have been difficult for people to picture using a smartphone. Now there's one in almost every pocket. Talking to an imaginary assistant sounded like a wild idea, but now many of us speak to them each day. The continued rise of AI will be similar. Even if a person doesn't understand AI now, they'll soon be using it for work or fun.

So, what does the future of AI look like?

Imagine a robot in every home that keeps us on schedule, readies us for school, cleans up, and feeds our pets. In 2024, Amazon made its first home robot, named Astro, available to the public. As of 2025, the seventeen-inch-tall robot was priced at $1,599. While the small, wheeled robot has limited capabilities now (it can't climb stairs), future models are guaranteed to do more.

The Tesla Bot, a machine that resembles and moves like a human, was announced in 2021. While currently in its testing phase, this robot will perform household chores, play with children, or provide companionship for the elderly.

The Tesla Bot

Robotics company Boston Dynamics has been hard at work on AI-powered bots designed to navigate dangerous environments on search and rescue missions. Imagine a herd of small doglike robots sent out following an earthquake or tornado. These robots would explore without fear to find and rescue people in need.

AI will become common in doctor's offices and hospitals to test blood samples for diseases. Results from these tests will be available in seconds instead of weeks. The sooner we know what's making us ill, the faster we can receive treatment.

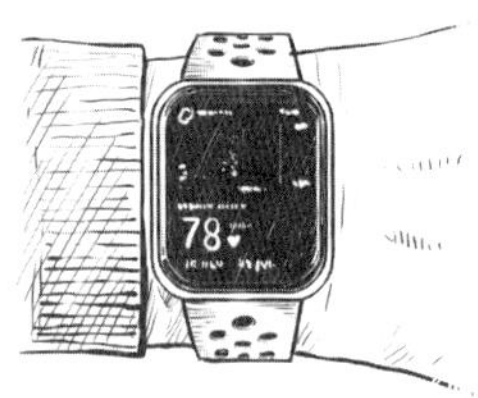

Wearable technology, such as the Apple Watch or fitness trackers, will continue growing in popularity. Decorative jewelry will contain tiny electronics to monitor our heart rates and body temperature. If they detect signs of illness, an alert will be sent to the user's phone—maybe even straight to their doctor. If AI detects that its wearer has fallen, it might automatically call for an ambulance.

AI will help us monitor microscopic levels of activity within our own bodies, as well as distant planets and possibly even far-off galaxies.

AI has been on Mars since NASA's Curiosity rover landed on the Red Planet in 2012. Nine years later, it was joined by the Perseverance rover. Both rovers carry similar AI instruments that help these car-size machines study rocks on the planet's surface. The AI determines which rocks to study and cracks them open with lasers to learn about the minerals inside.

NASA's rovers explore Mars with the help of AI. Once scientists on Earth choose where they want the rovers to go, the AI uses mounted cameras to find the safest path there. The future of space travel may not require humans at all.

SpaceX, founded by Tesla's Elon Musk, has shown us amazing things that space rockets can do with AI. Computers have helped spacecraft dock at the International Space Station and guided rockets back to specific landing points on Earth.

Autonomous AI–powered spacecraft could visit far-off planets to analyze their atmospheres. Hundreds of tiny spacecraft, called "swarm robotics," could explore a planet together. They'd work as one unit, "speaking" to one another as they spread out to map the surfaces of other planets. These spacecraft might even discover new worlds.

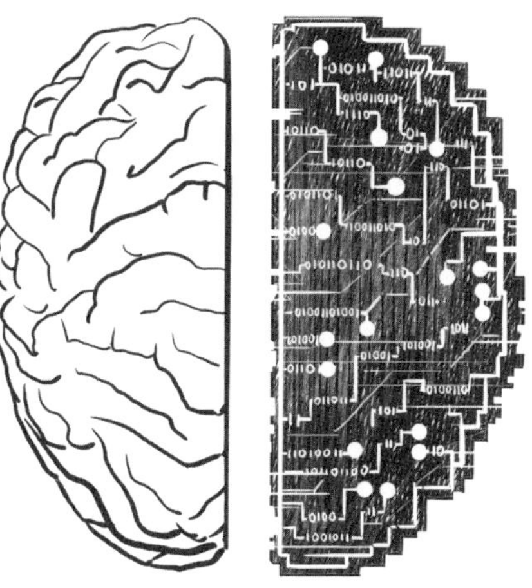

Artificial intelligence may not yet be smarter than a human being, but it's almost a certainty that one day, the electronic brain will rival our own.

Timeline of AI

1822 — Mathematician Charles Babbage unveils his difference engine, the first machine to compute math problems

1936 — Code-breaker Alan Turing creates the Turing machine to assist in solving difficult equations

1941 — German engineer Konrad Zuse reveals the Z3, the world's first programmable digital computer

1950 — Turing establishes the Turing test to challenge a computer's intelligence

1955 — Computer scientist John McCarthy coins the term "artificial intelligence"

1964 — MIT computer scientist Joseph Weizenbaum creates ELIZA, the first AI to gain widespread attention

1997 — Deep Blue defeats Russian chess grandmaster Garry Kasparov

2010 — Siri is released by SRI International

2011 — IBM's Watson AI defeats Brad Rutter and Ken Jennings on *Jeopardy!*

2014 — Tesla's Model S automobile becomes the first car to offer an "autopilot" mode

2017 — The Asilomar Principles, guidelines for the creation of future AI systems, are introduced

2024 — Amazon makes its home robot, Astro, available to the public

Timeline of the World

1822 — Charles Graham of New York receives the US patent for porcelain false teeth

1936 — Jesse Owens wins four gold medals in the Summer Olympics held in Berlin, Germany

1941 — The United States enters World War II after the Imperial Japanese Navy Air Service launches a surprise attack on the Pearl Harbor Naval Base on the coast of Oahu, Hawaii

1950 — Walt Disney's animated film *Cinderella* premieres in theaters

1955 — Rocker Elvis Presley makes his first television appearance

1964 — Activist and future South African president Nelson Mandela is sentenced to life in prison, but is released in 1990

2010 — Burj Khalifa, the world's tallest skyscraper at 163 stories, opens in Dubai

2011 — In Christchurch, New Zealand, an earthquake measuring 6.3 in magnitude kills 185 people

2014 — Scientists discover water vapor on the dwarf planet Ceres, located in the large asteroid belt between Mars and Jupiter

2024 — An ancient city that may have supported up to one hundred thousand people is discovered in the rainforest of Ecuador

Bibliography

***Books for young readers**

Negishi, Michiro. ***My Cell Phone Can Think: A Textbook on Artificial Intelligence, Second Edition***. Milford, CT: Neuroverb, 2018.

Ramge, Thomas. ***Who's Afraid of AI? Fear and Promise in the Age of Thinking Machines***. New York: The Experiment, 2019.

*Shukla, Neha. ***A Kids Book About AI***. Portland, OR: A Kids Co., 2023.

Wooldridge, Michael. ***A Brief History of Artificial Intelligence: What It Is, Where We Are, and Where We Are Going***. New York: Flatiron Books, 2021.